A NOTE ON THE WORD 'SELAH'

The Hebrew word *selah* (pronounced *SEE-luh* or *Seh-LAA*) appears frequently as a musical interlude in the Psalms and thrice in the book of Habakkuk. Its exact meaning is elusive. *Selah* is often translated: 'stop and consider'. Other interpretations of the word range from 'silence' to 'dance break'. The word only occurs in poetic and meditative contexts.

Here, *selah* finds an alternative translation in the migration of a hip movement across the Atlantic. *Dance.* Here it also means the briefest of human connections formed in transit. *Stop; consider.* It is also found in the ambivalent feelings aroused by a protest march or a newspaper column. *Silence.* The prayers and praise songs hiding under a lover's bed. The lost language of our parents, briefly revealed in the shape of a frown. *Selah.* Here possibilities cross borders, and even planets, in a playful search for meaning, and, although the precise nature of the word is difficult to pinpoint, we must surely wind back to music, reflection and loss.

Selah

Keith Jarrett

Burning Eye

Burning Eye Books
Never Knowingly
Mainstream

This edition published by Burning Eye Books 2017

www.burningeye.co.uk

@burningeyebooks

Burning Eye Books
15 West Hill, Portishead, BS20 6LG

ISBN 978-1-909136-96-0

Selah

CONTENTS

*'No matter how far away you walk from the church,
the prayer never leaves you.'*

Toni Stuart

ACKNOWLEDGMENTS

We who have survived.

We who have queered, fagged and poofed our way through the school system
　　　　we the survivors of oppressive institutions
　　　　　　　and of the sticklers and stonehearts that run them.

We who have survived
we with glitterproof ribs that once caved under the shadows
of our parents' disapproval
　　　　　　　we with pockets made of hand-me-down wounds

we of purse lips and handbag humour and zone 4, 5 & 6 commutes
we who once knew these streets by their bus shelters
　　　who still know these streets by their old names:
　　　　　　　Racism Road, Homophobia Grove, Bigot Hill

we who know history's desire to repeat
who know progress is neither linear nor neat.

　　　　We who do not take for granted.

*

10

We who have survived
the gentrifier's claw
    who have seen our media our companies our governments
        parade around rainbow flags and *Diversity* awards
            at their fashionable convenience

we who have journeyed past this cluster of colonising avenues
who have learned to sip heavily-accented wine
    who have washed our tongues in its morning after
we have loved beyond borders as we do not fear the other
    though fear is not foreign to us

we who were born on an island
and whose parents were born   on another island
    we have learned to build bridges
        we have learned to cross those bridges
            even as they burn with the fuel the politicians provided.

We who never take for granted.
We who stand in love and in fury and in power.

        Selah.

HIP-HOP SALVATION

They call me D. I tell them D is for *don* is for *done know!*
I invent rapalacious dismissals at the back of my class
and spend my lunchtimes at the school shop chomping
words at almost anyone who will listen

my Coke bottle is my mic, its contents my ignition
I drop bars after bars about this Walthamstow school
which doesn't quite fit me, like my low-hanging jeans
which wear me around the knees

I am possessed by the need to be freed by my words
because *word is bond* and in the beginning was the Word
(can I get a *word*?)

on Sundays, I swap my *F* words for hallelujahs
there, they call me *Dat Bwoy is Bless, you know!*
I am *Demon Destroyer*, and in my spiritual battles
I spit my rhymes over Redman instrumentals:

Let's talk spiritual, God's love unconditional towards us
Insomuch that he came from heaven just to die for us…
Look up in the sky, is it a bird, is it a plane?
No, it's Jesus Christ, he's coming back to save us again

back row friends' smirks let me break it down
with ragga chat to bring in my Caribbean congregation:
Satan is a born liar and him middle name is sin
Where we a go put him? Inna de Biffa bin!

there's a thinning line between Sunday and schooldays
and on Monday, some people still call me *Dawg*
as I have learned to growl and bark like DMX
but back in class, I turn tasks into rap, even in French:

La vie scolaire ce ne me suffit
Parce que nous savons l'education est une escroquerie
Nous sommes intelligents mais les profs ne le sont pas
Sauf Mademoiselle Green, bien sur

I slur through vocab excavated from *Tricolore*
and the *Larousse* dictionary for I am a text
book hip-hop nerd with a triple identity:

part wannabe rudie with fake Hilfiger baseball top
part pinstriped pulpit preacher in our Ilford church
part model pupil, turning tables on teachers' tasks

and they still call me D as I don't know how
to step into a full-grown name
and own it.

A NEW SPELLING OF MY NAME

title after Audre Lorde

For my birthday they rescued my name from a bargain
bucket in Barking, too cheap to afford a new one

dog-eared and ragged they wiped it down best
they could, said I was an old soul anyway.

I would have been a Lindsay Russell Daniel
or Kurtis, but they gave me this one to suckle on

so I chewed kicked bit and rattled it
till it tinkled jazz piano lullabies on my baby stool

I carried it to school on my shoulder. My friends called it
Jarrett the Parrot (Keith the) Chief and Mellow Man

it was the way its yellow eyes shut on top of class desks
I guess it was because it lacked focus

older now it became a pet I couldn't bear
to hear barked out on buses

I tried to drown it in the River Thames
it still skulked behind like a bad wind

my name was too dirty too old
and too much like my father

at home I was LK Junior Daniel D
and anything but   my name

but my name got bigger and grew claws
stretched to 5'8" tall and became solidly built

it swallowed me up and belched proudly
leaving me where I still remain: trapped inside

my name
          is now writing poetry last I heard

tells tall tales about its origins

far from the land of its adopted parents
far from the bric-a-brac lining East London streets

it can be found tracing its roots back to some old
Celtic village where it once meant something.

TICK

It's the first time I go alone to get my hair cut
and I want a tick that says *Welcome to the nineties*
that says *Talk to the tick 'cause the face ain't listening*
that says I am ten years old, big enough to bus myself
down Chingford Road to the market shops and
Changing Faces where Choice FM is cackling
through the tower speakers in the corner.

I wait on the burgundy leatherette settee
which has rips the shape of ongoing rows
and I am squashed between four sets of legs
and *big man talk* which bounces over my hood
while the endless buzz of three pairs of clippers
scrapes seamless fades into familiar scalps.

I want a phat scoop of *wicked!* on my head
that contrasts with my itchy three-striped shell suit
Auntie Rita sent over in a parcel from Florida
I want a bold bald patch tattooed onto the back
of my regulation short-back-'n'-sides.

A thick line divides the *chosen* from the geeks
a tick will convert me from a zero to a *don*
with just one small nod to the man in the mirror
now brandishing the machine above my head.

The seven pounds in change are whispering *Just. Do. It.*
but as I start to mouth the words the barber raises a hand.
Don't get no ideas. Your brother called me already.

I beg for a side parting. Anything that will get me one up
on my best friend Antoine.

I leave with one tiny line
                              (and that is all).

MIRROR

Knock knock. Year 8 girl raps on staffroom door.
She asks me to write about what I see in my mirror.
That's easy! I say. *I can do it in two words*: my dad.

But at dawn, when toothpaste stains and shower fog
are not enough to cover up my dad, more arrives
in lines I do not share with my young poetry class.

I do not say I spy a half-open tower block
overseeing my bathroom *bogle* dance
and a half-grey blanket tucking in behind the city.

I say I see a mirror: a flat wipe-clean surface.
I see the day ahead: a flat wipe-clean surface.
I see my shaved head: a flat wipe-clean surface.

I see history. *You stubborn like your granddad*, Mum says.
Him, born in Maroon town, where revolt and revolution
brought freedom for the few (& the rest remained chained).

My face frames the morning, beyond last night. And how I
stuffed my cheeks late with the bass from my portable
speakers shaking it, shake it, *Shake it like you mean it!*

My energy fizzes and now I see stars. I am King
of the Bathroom sliding off the tiles, sliding, dancing
king. I see a toothpaste grin. I beam wild.

Then I close my eyes, and it is still.

DISTINCTION
(**father**//mother)

A few weeks after the nation gauges the distinction between avoidance and evasion and I am gearing up for Jamaica with a wheel-worn suitcase and my father finally reveals the name of his birth town and it diminishes in my ear as he advises me not to venture there warning of my aunt who was chased back to the car and I imagine the townspeople as machete-wielding warriors fending off all her foreign for she is no longer their own and the town is hidden from the maps but the apartment I have rented for the week lies at the foot of the turning that twists you up the hills and down into my ancestry which is not signposted on the highway but I automatically veer towards it and my curiosity has once again ignited but the car I hired is Chinese and they have switched the steering panel over so every time I try to signal the windscreen wipers brush me away and when I let the search engine take me there instead I count three Jarretts in the first article and the first man pictured has the same stubborn eyes I used to think belonged to my mum's side // at the roadside I flag a route taxi to the bus station then a coach to Kingston and then Halfway Tree and at Spanish Town I experience cousin Junior for the first time and his eyes shift left right indicating the cab to my aunt's house and the distance is measured in the sideway glances I have seen my mother make and I forget how much city is in my mother and how little she tells of it save that she was baptised in the capital in a Chinese church whose name she skips and a sixth passenger enters and the driver fixes a look in the rear-view mirror that closes the door and no one talks till a phone rings and I clutch mine which is on silent and do not ask the name of the neighbourhood as thirty minutes of road squint back at me and I avoid looking at my cousin's scar which bends and fades like the tarmac to dirt and when we have exhausted our journey I do not ask for water but my aunt offers me a smile and some photographs which I sip quickly and when I recount this to my mother later as she chokes back questions I forget to leave out the two miles I walked that night along the highway when I jumped out the taxi too soon.

PSALMS 133: A SONG OF ACCENTS

They say my language   broken
because I burst through the skin

of a tambourine
and my tongues never come

fast enough   that tarrying night
I did born

They say my speech   broke
short-sleeve tongue   greased

with the sweaty palm of a Praying
Mother. My beard is full of ointment

the skirts of my garments
trail down to the Thames estuary

the Atlantic swallowed my vowels
and I am speaking on borrowed blood.

*Cleansing, cleansing, cleansing stream
I see. I plunge.* I decolonise.

They say my language is borrowed
was never returned

tambourine skin can't fix again
send me a chorus, Lord.

RESONANCES

for the Royal Festival Hall Organ celebrations, 2014

I. Invocation
Here's the church and here's the steeple   a chorus of fingers
with the press of a switch   doors released
breath held in tin and lead vessels is freed
to voice sound: *open the pathways.*

II. Tacky's revolt – Jamaica, 1760
A note resonates through time   through reed-tongue pipe
bending the ear of a man I imagine   standing as tall as cane
resting briefly in the abeng of his rebellion   staved off by backra's whip and gun.
Pull. Stop.

III. Ska migration – London, 1950s
After a war, note clings desperately to hip newly-come rhythm skanks
off into blues bar   and scores become unsettled   peal away
and same organ used to swell the night's white noise with black notes
fills hired halls with Pentecostal fire across the Thames   come Sunday.

IV. Solo – London, 2014
Ask me how much it hurts on a scale   of one to eight thousand
my answer is in song   I too draw my breath from these resonances:
Bach, Glass, Studio One.   I, too, a piece of history's crooked smile covered over now.

V. Benediction
A great organ takes about as long to build as a battleship
but we don't mention the cabinet   and the closeted beast lurking
killing time   before the world ends, not in fire or ice or trumpets sounding
but in the mouth of this god   of lead, tin, copper, bones and blood.

abeng: *an animal horn or musical instrument in the Twi (Ghanaian) language, used in Jamaica by Maroons
(escaped   slaves) to communicate.*
backra: *slaveholder.*
*A great organ takes about as long to build as a battleship: from the Royal Festival Hall Official (written in
association with London County Council), 1951.*

21

SWEET THING

(for Black History Month exhibition, Walthamstow Library, 2012)

Out of Sugar
One Bitter History; and one tonne alone provides
enough wanton speculative sweet-tooth minds with the
energy to churn the cogs of City-trader floors; eyes sparkle
with this crystal commodity; dock-warehouses stocked with cubes as
wide as Empire; entire nations built on bend-back blade, blade burns in hands as well
while the swell of cane propels ships around the refined world, as
buy and sell takes hold and households nip and break the
loaves, graded in worth by shade. And now the taste
is a sweet solution; cane fields equals *quids in*
Out of Sugar, champagne.

Text going vertically down on the right-hand side taken from Narrative: Sugar from the West Indies.

22

AND ANOTHER SWEET THING

(Rose Hall, Jamaica, June 2016)

Even though the gaps between my teeth are laced with stringy
even though the gap between the fence reveals a pile of fallen
fruit even though the gaps between this draft
and the previous draft

> included a whole interlude
> where I tried to scrub the juice stain from my shirt
> to find an adequate metaphor for my family history
> but I failed and it all seeped through

and while it is the season
and while the Caribbean Sea grabs my ankles like an anxious child
and while I know one day these waters will rearrange themselves
and rise up against its borders

> and the gap between *this* draft and the last
> involved discovering my name in a paragraph
> in a chapter on the history of Montego Bay
> via a 1655 settler named Colonel Nicholas Jarrett
> an English patriot whose descendants still remain

and though I am sucking on this new strand of information
and though my hand is full of middle fingers and digger thumbs
and though I know how the tree was introduced from India
and into the other colonies by the Portuguese – uprooted, if you will –

I still cannot give space to this exoticised fruit, conscious as I am
to not satisfy the reader's hunger for bucolic descriptions
of coastal sunrises and cool breeze and itchy sand

> but perhaps not extending to the ants
> reclaiming all the flesh
> left sticking to the knife. A colony of ants
> appearing so fast, so fast.

HOARDER
(I AM BECOMING MY GRANDDAD)

dedicated to 'Dad' Jarrett, RIP

My granddad, with a vague finger, directs me towards the bathroom door: in the cupboard, behind the ironing board, halfway up from the floor, on a wood shelf, in a carrier bag, are a pair of matched socks. The nurse waits at Granddad's bandaged feet, his diabetic rot another ailment he endures, while I search through rows of bags, tins, and useful things, unused since he and Grandma moved here ten years ago.

In their Essex bungalow, even at this cupboard door, I always find myself underneath a *God Bless This House* sign – a Jamaica-shaped wood carving nailed at an awkward angle. Inside, cases full of *just-in-case* buttons, bed sheets and bills press against each other; leads dangle like roots I could stretch all the way back to my own flat, a long, infrequent train ride away.

Later, below my bedsit doorway, my lopsided bus sign nailed above, I observe the bag of odd socks weighing down my bed, and a plastic crate full of receipts, poetry flyers and postcards. Starting with the socks, I breathe in hard and tip the whole pile in the bin – one by open-mouthed one, these puppeteers' playthings – because I don't want to become him. Yet.

And I'm not talking about his legs, or how his longsuffering nature makes him suffer more than his fair share, nor am I talking about his slow, meandering stories:

> *You know my cousin Peter – the one over in Canada? You know I went to Canada back – how many years it was, love? Yes, I know you did ask after him – yes, I never even see him for must be twenty years now – is how old you is again? Bwoy, time no fly no more, time just gone! I member when your daddy tell me seh you coming out the hospital, you was only this big you know! Yes, love, I know I sen over the pictures and you still never forgive me for that – every time I mention my cousin name! Anyway, your –hold on – is he your great-uncle? No, your cousin once, no, twice removed, the*

*both of we grew up in a place called Falmouth, and we did
go up to the school...*

He draws from a full bag of life history. I mean all the things he
stores in carrier bags in boxes including the one pair of clean,
matching socks he thinks will impress his visitor, things he cannot
throw. I hope to keep my own feet light, for now. But I know one
day they too will bandage my leg and say my name real slow.

DANCE: ETU/ECHÚ

In Jamaican Etu, feet must stay close to the ground to maintain contact with the ancestors. In Cuba, Echú, spirit of chaos and trickery, is the counterpart to Elegguá, opener of pathways.

Because they never have nowhere to bury my
navel string, I just born to fly. My feet don't tie

so good to the ground. The move-ment drum dictate
don't fit my way-ward spirit and so I hesitate

on the monitoring form too. I mostly tick *Other*
Carib-BEE-an or *Ca-RIB-bean*? I never bother

how I spit the ribs of my history. I am chaos by any name:
Whaapen bredda? Or *Qué pasa, 'mano*? It all the same

but see I just skip an island and now my hips tight-
up in an alter-native way. Just make me shift my right

leg, watch this irreverent shaker sing up someplace
to belong. Now hear me keep possession of this song.

PSALMS 139: THE LAST TIME MY MOUTH WAS DETAINED BY CUSTOMS

after Imani Cezanne

*

it had been speaking too well
or too slow
frowning too hard
while intoning the national anthem
in the wrong key

it held more than one song inside it

**

did you pack this mouth yourself?
your breath smells of mourning
are there any decomposing
family members inside?
you cannot carry these undocumented vowels

who gave you these words?

***

God of blue glove
God of scanner wand
who has searched me and known
how well I have folded
these unsmiling frontiers
can't you see how I have steadied
all my inflections?

I prostrate myself
in immigration
before you

I lift my hands above my head
in praise.

AIN'T NO BLACK IN THE UNION JACK [1]

but in my magnanimity I am able to forgive
what is, arguably, an administrative error.

> [the oversight shakes hands with the overseer]

Indeed, flag-making was never one's forte –
I, more predisposed to epistemology
am vigorously verifying track changes
in the wide margins of history.

> [to marginalise is to invite annotation] [2]

And the footnote, ultimately, justifies the text,[3]
and the textile factory has long since out-
sourced its staff, and the tricoloured fabric
they promised would soon tear at the seams

> [rivers of riot, waves of bloody bandages] [4]

has held – although shakily – thus far. Thus far
despite engaging in online interdisciplinary fora [5]
where robust debate can be located on this matter
the empty signifier of our present condition
proffers no resolution to this ribboning polemic.

---

1 Racial taunt used in the playground towards the end of the
twentieth century; also the title of a book on Black British culture.

2 Spivak (1988) – and many others since – argues for a reframing of
narratives related to agency and subalternity; here, we argue more
for a repositioning of the lens, i.e. 'speaking back' to power.

3 Ibid, 31. See also: Fanon, Gilroy, Hall, hooks, CLR James...
(extended bibliography to follow).

4 See Enoch Powell's 1968 address (commonly called 'Rivers of
Blood'), referenced in multiple discourses on immigration,
social integration and racism in Britain. Here 'wave' serves a dual
purpose, subverting Powell's speech while also signalling flag-
related language.

5 Despite multiple warnings to the tune of 'Do not feed the trolls',
curiosity has led the author to navigate his research to the more
rebarbative arenas of popular comment websites.

[a half-mastered argument]

Furthermore, it would be expedient to re-orient
problematisation of flags and colour representation
into the wider discourse of (sub)liminal space
being cautious of those who seek finial solutions.

POEM POEM IV (TRIGGER)

Trigger warning
because this is a poem
where the lion dies

call him *Cecil Mufasa Aslan...*
but don't call him after anyone
who cannot breathe
inside police chokeholds
inside the barrel of a gun
inside the symbolism which isn't lost
on me nor on the man
(it's always a man, right?)
who asks below the line
why there isn't a white
history month and a straight
pride and why these reverse
patriarchal ~~communists~~ columnists
are writing these mean
things all the time

I can't finish this poem
while my anger still can't fit
into these jeans
so I am stacking up
on wild locusts and honey
from Wholefoods
(not cheap these days)
and my basket is empty
and my basket runs
over like a wilderness
inside the lone voice of a prophet.

(NOW WASH YOUR HANDS)

When the riots come / with passports as silver-blue as
cockroaches / squeezing through the pulled-down blinds / in
the half-sleep of our bedrooms / and thus

when they park their oversized luggage in our living rooms /
upturning the wastepaper baskets / burning the bookshelves /
the bushes / the silences / the anthems

from the radio and / when they blow smoke rings through our
pillows / while our fathers' hands swarm with mirrors and guns
and no longer work in tandem

our mothers will sing / *But we were once the riots, child! / we*
were once the drowned / the dreamed-up beast / the damned
/ and then

our mothers will wring the riots from our blood / while our
fathers curse and prophesy outside / and we will eat its
aftermath / and the riots will multiply within us

BACKWARDS (AFTER A DROWNING)

after Wallace Stevens

*'Some of our towns are festering sores, plagued by
swarms of migrants and asylum seekers, shelling out
benefits like Monopoly money. Make no mistake, these
migrants are like cockroaches.'*

Katie Hopkins, *The Sun*

13. I become a sparrow.

12. *Consider the sparrow in its simplicity!*

11. The search engine cannot name that feeling inside of me –
complacency? Complicity? Its shadow weighs the night down
into day.

10. Power lives in a locked-up house on a street with no name.
I remember things with names can be dismantled.

9. *Praise be the respected columnist!* We give thanks for her
powerful writing on this matter.

8. *Oh wretched* — ! Amusement is in the process of colonising
my chest. Asylum was never granted for my anger.

7. Today He announces the closure of all His borders. *The very
hairs on my head* —

6. I have been praying to a foreign god.

5. We have been singing the song of cockroaches. We have
been drowning for 500 years. *Olokun, watch over them.*

4. I try to hold my body as a boulder, I try to sound out my
new national anthem: *I'm forever blowing bubbles* – I remain
stateless.

3. I notice how, when I am drunk, the borders blur. We are one.

2. When I wake late and read my notes, I will stumble at the place I wrote: *history's open-handed slap to its children.* I will not keep that line. *History* has another name. *Drink on these things.*

1. This spring, when we learn about the drowned bodies, I offer my sleep to the yawning comments. I do not search the night for validation below the editorial line. I clasp the words of Baldwin and King, knowing that wretched speech is no worse than negative peace. I resist. Reverse the narrative.

A PLACE IN THE SUN (WITH TONSILLITIS)

My cousin says I've lost my keys for the third time this week because Venus is in retrograde. The real reason is because the thermometer's mercury has burst through the glass and I'm delirious. I'm watching season 2 of *Breaking Bad* and just don't get it. My tonsils are on fire. I've sent my entire unsupportive family to Coventry. I've paused the DVD to switch to TV and catch the end of *A Place in the Sun*.

Two doctors, sick of the housing bubble, seek an alternative to their overpriced Battersea bedsit. The TV presenter suggests Mercury (the planet) and the couple, humourless, suggest she should be first in line to burn. A bottle of factor 5000 lotion later, she says it's unseasonably cool there lately but will take no risks. She flicks her wrists to retrieve the keys to the BBC's flying saucer. She has *just* the property but it's a wildcard.

The couple, a hard sell, spend the whole journey comparing commutes and rolling their eyes, until they arrive on the rock, a stone's throw away from the home of *that dead star*. The presenter, while reverse parking, lists some perks about the *Iron Planet*: early retirement, a birthday every eighty-eight days (the two men are horrified). *I just want you to be open-minded,* she says. *You artistic types* (they're doctors) *are fabulous at gentrifying places and this is a pure untapped goldmine with the highest eccentricity in our solar system – listen, let me level with you. Earth hasn't been all it's cracked up to be: the future is Mercury.*

The presenter sips my Lucozade and it fizzes down my throat. Earth really isn't what it cracked up to be: the empires are crumbling; politicians are greedy; the musicians are broke, or no good; the people are ignorant; the poets are found wanting; Mercury is rising.

The presenter drips down my head and wrings out my tongue before continuing her spiel. *You may find this surprising, but the moon landing was fake* (the doctors clear their throats nervously), *half-baked humans tap their desires into electronic devices, while half-baked poets make half-hearted attempts to compensate for only – why don't you pack your stuff and pick a sunspot right here? The future isn't orange, it's fifty-eight-day-long days and no seasons with an orbital range of 46–70 million kilometres from the sun...*

The couple walk away to explore, mid-speech. The camera follows as they bicker about the budget. The camera pans out on the acres of space. The couple blur till they're just a dot on the screen.

Sweat drips from every pore in my head. The camera zooms to the pursed-lipped presenter. And as my eyes start to close, I can see her tiptoeing back, ever-so-carefully, to the comfort of her publicly-funded flying saucer.

MAKING LIGHT: HOW WE BROKE UP (SCRIPT)

[scene 1]
on the first take, the light is all wrong and the lines
are stale and the lover feeds them to the protagonist
but he cannot make a scene at the table, & filming runs over

[scene 2]
cut to exterior: sparking a cigarette the lover speaks
of film heroes, one of the leads is called earth, right?
green and yellow. another detonates the device

Note:
I grew up with my eyes behind my fingers
so I know there are thirty seconds to spare
and the hero's hands are trembling
and I know real life isn't like this because:

a)   the countdown in the grey of his eyes didn't always work properly
b)   I didn't always know which part of my tongue I should cut
c)   sometimes things just need to blow up

[scene 3]
in this one, I still don't get to be the hero

[scene 4]
in this one, neither do you

[scene 5]
in the deleted scene, the constant bickering
leads up to the kiss after the cliffhanger
when he says *save yourself* as the barriers are coming down
and his leg is stuck

but the lover stays.

MERCURY

You are lying next to me
we are reciting MC Solaar:
dreaming the winds of Arizona
Les paroles perdus de Harry Zona…

it is Wednesday. *Mercredi.*
Eighty-eight days since I shrugged myself
single and I am here in a shrunken room
and you do not ask me what I am thinking

I am thinking of Icarus
because, lately, I've been burning to fly
and, sometimes, my desire for freedom
scorches a hole in my bed

so I am imagining that flying *is* burning
and I spark another half-crushed cigarette
I've fished out from a mug on the floor
and hold it to your mouth

I am overly late again going somewhere
and I could use a pair of wingèd feet
or a smaller orbit
but on this particular Wednesday

all that matters are my sweaty armpits
your legs intertwined with mine
and the infinite stretching of time.

DANCE: BUTTERFLY

Today I spotted an orange
butterfly flapping nervously

between the loops hanging
from the rail of the Overground

train and the look passed between
my eyes and yours, our wings
touched and moved away again.

VENTRILOQUISM

Brompton Cemetery, November 2013

I. Ventriloquist *(for mi pana Fran)*

On the way to the hospital   a shortcut   through the long
shadows   of death
I fear no evil but the sharp   November wind
which snips through the lining of my Puffa coat

the sun's so low you could seize it with both hands   like a moment
it's weak against the light of the greying sky
dragging its frame over the tops of tombs

and in the distance
a man is entertaining a loud phone conversation
from the back of a gravestone   with faded lettering

and there's a predictable metaphor for God in there
precisely because I can't see him
precisely because I can't reach for it now in the face of sorrow

and it seems   in that moment
that he's speaking   for those who've passed on
perhaps   the gravest kind of ventriloquism

because before I approached it was dead   quiet
nothing but squelching leaves to punctuate   my thoughts.

II. Graveyard Shift

I hear the dusk used to gather men up here
for brisk encounters
crouching under bushes   by the crypts
and I won't pass comment

on the partnership between sex & death not exactly civil
when the two of them bicker   incessantly
at all the best black tie dinners
you never were invited to

going at each other's throats with the engraved silverware
(you have to work from the outside in, he says
amuse-bouche main   pudding   cheese)
snide *ahems* dished out like mustard   sparing but enough to clear
a   cold

call it a trick of dark   but the shadows
are pressing up against each other   hardening
and only two weeks ago
I was thinking my life from the far prong   of a distant fork

when you told me to consider   our future
a regurgitated speech   you intoned at the table
candles flickering at each end   of our perspectives
but now mine has turned sideways

and the gurning portrait I had   of myself
is rubbing out slowly   like words on a gravestone
my landscape now feasts on decaying leaves
while the trees' thin wings reach out   in supplication

and maybe I'm speaking for you now
but I can't snap back at this particular cold   and the warm
of a smile only lasts me this long   shorter each time
like the daylight

and because a lecturer once told me that dictionaries are graveyards
        for words
because writing is forgetting to live   because a tongue births
new meanings with each breath   with each twist
and sounds shift mouth to mouth

because of this I am writing my words   down
to bury my silence.

MAKING LIGHT: BAD BLOOD (EPILOGUE)

The nurse is emptying my blood into a tube
and the light
the light of her demeanour is unbearable
she is asking something about my lunch
and I'm trying not to feel ---------
while the tube keeps drinking red from my arm

The nurse is emptying me of blood
I want her to take it all away
so it doesn't have to keep bubbling up like this

Bad blood
Sit
Bad blood
Stay
Bad blood
Beg.

THE DAY I BOUGHT YOU FLOWERS

Tesco's. Discount rose.
Lucky girl! the cashier chimes.
I smile: *Yes, he is.*

A GAY POEM

They asked me if I had a gay poem
and I said, *straight up, no*
my poems don't deviate between straight lines
my poems don't *mince* their words
or bend, or make *queer* little observations

I mean, even presenting this question
puts me in a precarious position
and how would I broach the subject
with my own creation?

Like: *Excuse me – poem – are you gay?*
Have you grown up contrarily
to what I wanted you to say?
I mean, I certainly didn't write you that way –

maybe I should have peppered your verses
with sport, girls and beer
maybe I failed you –
or did another writer turn you queer?

Let's say, hypothetically, *this* poem is gay
maybe it's a confused poem
that just needs straightening out

maybe I could insert verses from Leviticus
speak over it in tongues, douse it in holy
water or give it a beat, beat, beat:
Batty poem fi dead! / Batty poem fi dead!
Rip up chi chi poem inna shred!

They asked me if I had a gay poem
but the truth is, I didn't know
until one of my own poems spoke up
and tapped me on the shoulder:

Look here, dad/author, I'm not confused
not alternative – and the words I choose
to marry with make me different
but not any less eloquent

the more your hatred tries to erase
the more your synonyms demean
the more you say you hate
the sinner and despise the sin

the more you try to clip my words
and stifle my expression
the more I know it's you, not me
who should be called into question.

EMOTIONAL CELLULITE
(A SONG OF GRIEF AND COURAGE)

'According to a new report, cellulite could be down to your state of mind. Here we ask whether those bumpy thighs really could be triggered by repressed stress...'
Grazia magazine, July 2013

[Hum after each question]
Do you suffer from emotional cellulite?
Are your chakras lopsided or incorrectly aligned?
Is your spirituality sagging? Is your third eye wrinkled?
Are you baggy around your relationship line?

> I wake up lonely because my bed
> has recently lost the weight
> of a nine-and-a-half-stone relationship.
>
> This beautiful room is empty.
> My suitcase is beach-ready.

Are there red circles on your self-image
that need to be diminished?
Are you a half-finished product
of your own disappointment?

> I am bench-pressing my way back
> into tighter T-shirts bursting with failure.

Are your love handles forming
a barrier to your creative success?
Do you feel bloated? Do you feel wanted?
Do you feel haunted? Are you exercising
your demons regularly?

> I am wrong for being born
> into this worn-out metaphor
> for survival, renewal, righteousness.
>
> I am a brick being thrown
> into the glass house of my body.

II
Who sells cellulite?

According to recent reports
cellulite may be caused by:

a) stress
b) repressed anger/creativity
c) a childhood spent watching *Police Academy 3* at Christmas, in
front of a dodgy fourteen-inch-screen TV where you, youngest of
four, were tasked with holding up the wire hanger aerial

> (and maybe the film was *Cliffhanger* and
> you watched it upside down
> and maybe you have been holding up
> dramas ever since).

According to a recent report cellulite is a sign
of the body responding to all that is negative around it:

this bad government/rising home prices/phallic skyscrapers
penetrating the red-angry sky/metal spikes shooting from the ground
like nuclear flowers/the violence of borders—

The cellulite-seller sells cellulite for sure...
the supermarket sells cellulite
the self-serving scanner sells cellulite
the emergency hammer is calling your name.

Who sells cellulite?
My body is a five-foot-eight
eighty-kilogram receptor for cellulite
the only thing that makes it lighter is love
love for the people who do not wish me silent or invisible.

I am more than this digitally-enhanced cellulite city.
I am a helium sparrow rising with friendship in my beak
and with a song in my blood
and with this blood in my rage.

PLAYING HIS MUSIC ON SHUFFLE
(OR HOW FRIEND *A* DESCRIBES THAT
CASUAL ENCOUNTER)

And then the inevitable happened: an unfortunately-timed
leaking of Clark Sisters, *Jesus is a love song, LOVE* – full-blown
hallelujah-style chorus he didn't even know he possessed
gospel-slapped the 2am night when he plugged in his phone.

And he still refers to it as *the accident:* he fled the man's home,
fearful of a god who punishes men who lie with men, blown
away by sinful desires, with eternal fire and Mary Mary; now
he builds lyricless lists, lays down each track before getting laid.

I think that probably makes him a considered lover but
I wonder if the real accident isn't his new electro playlist
but in the playground where he must downplay the full
range of his repertoire. His bed rocks to a tune of predictable.

I hope one day he uncovers the praise song in his bed frame.
I hope that day he learns to dance away his shame, with
a man who fears neither worship nor repentance.

HIGHLIGHTS OF THE OLD TESTAMENT

That day I tried to recall them all:
the children of the Edomites
who begot whom and with which concubines.

I drew red circles round the names
like they were cellulite in a gossip mag –
and then he was not.

I smote a few demons
from under the comfort of my quilt.
I reread Leviticus. Guiltless.

SELAH

After I have protested outside embassies
After I have bought badges and signed
petitions, wondering if my details will
land in guilty hands and *Shame on you!
Shame on you! Shame on you!* After I have
read, and seen red, and been ambiguous
After I have drained myself of pride and
piss in a discreet corner, over a drain,
and then, after I have been that drain
and after I have spilled my stories and
after I have once again pulled my tongue
from the custody of its thirsty mouth, and
after I have drunk and after I have been
promised living water and hellfire by
the same preachers and *Shame on you!
Shame on you!* preying on my lonely,
and then... after I thought that, if Jesus
couldn't save me maybe feminism would,
and after I burnt my bra quietly with my
chest still inside and after the smoke
inhalation and I have singed everything
and I can no longer pull myself out by my
short and curlies and I can no longer pull
myself out of the protest or pull myself
out of my bed of a morning

And after R Kelly, after learning I damn
well can't and after believing in myself
when I could no longer believe in truth or
flight and then believing in the divination
of tongues locked against each other
during one-night stands, and after
breaking my bed during an adventurous
handstand, and after vomiting in that
room and promising never to drink again
and after drinking again and not vomiting
and after vomiting again but not from
drinking and after returning to the broken
bed, and after the second coming, and
after erasing all the religious references
and downplaying all cultural contexts

and negating all the adverse effects of history to justify genocide and after I keep muttering: *History keeps repeating; history keeps repeating; history keeps repeating...* until my tongue is dry and after I have drunk again and after I have become a full-blown *slacktivist* and deliberately avoided the protest because I have no voice left to shout with and, consequently, after I have buried my tongue somewhere else instead and after I absent-mindedly wrote you a poem, after that... and after I burnt that poem and felt the hairs on my chest singe one more time and *Shame on you! Shame on you!* and I have forgotten how to roll back the progress of time and release the pressure on my head, which is always so angry, always gets rubbed up the wrong way by the well-meaning – because, after I have bartered some of my anger for vulgarity and some of my sadness for sarcasm and I still feel short-changed; and I mean *before*; I mean during these mean days when I have to endure the weight of a double-decker bus on my eyelids every single time I leave my home, and before the violence and before the drumbeat begins to really kick in and before my cry is drowned out by the bass and you forget I was even here I just wanted to say never look down.

WHEN THE ROLL IS CALLED

(for the Royal Festival Hall Organ celebrations, 2014)

So while wrecking balls are being ridden by pop stars
as if they were prize horses
and tools are being licked
and critics are sounding off about music –
or the pitiful lack of it in songs

and while half of Surrey is perpetually drowning
because of equal marriage and those two men
holding hands in the Macklemore music video
jumping off a cliff into a sea of convention

and while education is described in terms that render it
not so much a hot potato as it does a squished banana
lost at the bottom of a broken bag
to the tick-ticking sound of interference

I am standing in front of the machine of the apocalypse
composed of lead, tin, wood, voiceless copper, and ivory
flooding the hall with its 7,866 immigrant tongues
(and those are just the conservative figures)

I am standing in the middle of a fifty-nine-and-a-half-year-old
argument about Britishness/tradition/inclusiveness/discord
after pipes have been peddled from Durham to London and
hot air is being blown from the throne of this god to create song

I am standing inside a post-war celebration:
these tubes of defiant harmonies
upright like victory fingers

pointing: here is the church and here is the steeple
open the doors, open your ears, *open thou our lips*
for the sing-along theme tune

this machine was never meant to be handled neatly
just like history which, once studied, will always be revised
and music will always be a controversy
and the pedals will always set the tone

while the electro-pneumatic stops are pulled out
in combo moves; the organist is playing
Street Fighter on a noisy games console

but this isn't the time for sound bites
this is the time for high scores and broad churches
and minds stretched out to breaking point across
Waterloo Bridge, while the congregation is singing
from the same hymn book, burning with revolution

and in another fifty years of evolution and of song
this organ may still stand, when ambience, baroque,
classical, dance and dubstep have sidestepped into
the sidebars of history books and the scores have changed

a few octaves, and wrecking balls have demolished
old office blocks for shiny new towers
surrounding the Royal Festival Hall
(and some other genius politician has confused climate
change with basic human rights)

maybe I will not be standing here then
but, here, the air will still be pushed up to the sky
by somebody's deft fingers and feet

and the Quintadena, Clarion, Diapason, Sesquialtera, Tierce,
Rohrnazard, Gedackt, Dulzian, Bombarde,
Trumpet, Cromorne, Hautboy,
Viola, Celeste
and Vox Humana

will all answer their names when the roll is called

                        and that will be all.

BEFORE YOU LEAVE/BENEDICTION

let there be light in all thirty-two
of your rooms, put your gospel
on shuffle and maximise your tinnitus
pluck open the stiff windows, stick your
tongue outside, put the kettle on and
shake it off again, call *that* a black coffee
breathe
                    before you leave
forget where you are going
remember *you* are the destination
welcome yourself to you.
Population: one
your shadow has no suffrage
least not in this blooming town
                    before you leave
burn all your lucky charms
and give the smoke a wet kiss
and if you must, pack my words
into a fist, twist them into flowers
gift them to the violence of the night
lay them backwards, three times
over your doorposts, layer them over
each other to insulate your walls
forgive them for they have thinned
                    if you must
remember these streets end someplace
so face the music if you can feel it
allow your wide, raging strides
to fall soft between the beats
if you're not too embarrassed
                    sing
remember all that is sweet
think on these things

now, go.

MAKING LIGHT: ABSENCE (EPILOGUE)

Love,

the sky was foul this morning
piled high with clouds, with noise, with air
the wrong kind of sunless air that just keeps
on coming, slapping me about the face
and I was hoping it would clear by lunch
but why should it?

All those years I wanted to be Gideon
just to hold on to the sun all day
but God only seems to favour those who fight
and I was busy scooping away my thirst
with bloodless hands
when they were distributing arms.

*

Love,

in the absence of you
I am hugging these waters close.

I know things will become clear with time:
whether I will lap it with my tongue
or sing it as a psalm.

Something has lifted.

THANK YOUS

This bit is almost harder than writing the poems themselves! I have so many people I could thank but I'll try to keep this brief...

Thanks Clive Birnie and the Burning Eye team for your patience and for believing in this collection. Thanks and big up to my Spoken Word Educator buddies, especially Raymond Antrobus, Dean Atta and Indigo Williams who have been a rock in dark times. Those who saw some of the poems here when they were sketchy: Matt Beavers, James Carey, Mark Harris, Nic Jarrett, Rob Lucas, James McKay, Paula Varjack. To Hannah Lowe for amazing editorial help. A special big up to Malika Booker and Peter Kahn who were time-generous and honest where it was needed. The Unwriteables, my workshop buddies, who keep me in check. The spoken word community in London and beyond, who breathe life – and urgency – into poetry. To so many more who inspire me to become a better poet, a better person.

Keith Jarrett writes poetry and short fiction and is a former London and UK Poetry Slam Champion. He runs workshops, and has performed at and co-ordinated poetry festivals in the UK and abroad, in English and Spanish.

Keith's five-star reviewed poetry show *Identity Mix-Up* debuted at the Edinburgh Fringe festival in 2013. Subsequently, he completed the pioneering Spoken Word Educators programme – the first of its kind in the world – teaching in a secondary school while studying for a Writing in Education MA at Goldsmiths University.

He is a winner of several slams, including the Rio International Poetry Slam championship at the FLUPP favela literary festival (Brazil, 2014) and the Calabash slam (Jamaica, 2016). He was also a Fiction Fellow at Lambda Writers' Retreat in Los Angeles in 2015 and his debut poetry pamphlet, *I Speak Home* (Eyewear), was also released that year.

Keith was named as a Spread the Word LGBT Hero in 2017. He was also listed under the BBC's New Talent Hotlist after being commissioned to write a monologue, performed at the Old Vic theatre and filmed for BBC Four in the summer.

Since being awarded a PhD studentship at Birkbeck University of London, Keith is now researching the culture of Caribbean Pentecostalism in London and, as *Selah* went to press, he was completing his first novel.

...gates wi... something new – namely his bla... ingredients such as migrant parents, a religious upbringing and living in inner city London. His poetry dances an awkward shuffle as he negotiates and seeks to reconcile what he inherits from his Caribbean roots, what he has lost and who he is becoming on this British island. The poems are fraught with relationships shaped by a severing that creates a limbo where Jarrett states:

> *My body is a boulder, I try to sound out my new*
> *national anthem: I am forever blowing bubbles – I remain stateless.*

Here the poems are songs that testify, praise, lament and pray, drawing heavily on biblical imagery, mythology and language to score the relevant notes for his compositions. His elegiac pieces are epigraphic whether written for a diabetic dying grandfather or about the breakdown of a long-term relationship. This new black British voice is relevant and necessary."

Malika Booker

Burning Eye Books £9.99
ISBN 978-1-909136-96-0

9 781909 136960

www.burningeye.co.uk